WHAT CAN I SEE in the DESERT?

Annabel Griffin

illustrated by Rose Maclachlan

HUNGRY TOMATO™

First published in Great Britain in 2021
by Hungry Tomato Ltd
F1, Old Bakery Studios,
Blewetts Wharf, Malpas Road
Truro, Cornwall, TR1 1QH, UK

A CIP catalog record for this book is available from the British Library.

ISBN 978-1-913440-11-4

Manufactured in the USA

Discover more at:
www.hungrytomato.com

CONTENTS

Words in bold capital letters **LIKE THIS** can be found in the glossary.

WHAT CAN I SEE IN THE DESERT?

There is so much to see in these dry and scorching places. Can you spot the animals and plants that make their home in the desert?

MAJESTIC BEASTS

These large animals have all ADAPTED to survive a long time without water.

Got the hump?

Camels store water and energy in their humps as fat. This means that they can go a long time without eating or drinking.

A rare sight

The addax is **ENDANGERED**. There are only a few left living in the wild.

Long distance travelers

In the desert, elephants will walk up to 50 miles a day in search of food.

KEEPING IT COOL

REPTILES are **COLD-BLOODED**, which means they can't control their body temperature. Most of them spend a lot of time in **BURROWS** to try to keep cool.

A super long lie-in!

Box turtles **HIBERNATE** for over half the year.

Shaking off danger

Rattlesnakes use their rattles to make loud noises to scare off **PREDATORS**.

Mighty monsters

These are the largest lizards living in the United States.

Thirsty?

Desert Tortoises can survive a whole year without drinking any water!

Desert devil

This strange looking creature is covered in spikes to help protect itself.

FEATHERED FRIENDS

Take a look at these amazing desert birds! They all live and act in very different ways.

Clever nesting

Gila Woodpeckers often make their homes in cacti.

World's largest bird

Ostriches can grow up to nine feet tall.

Tasty leftovers

Vultures are **SCAVENGERS**, which means they eat animals that are already dead.

Night owls

Great Horned Owls are **NOCTURNAL**. They sleep in the day and hunt at night.

Kicking up dust

Roadrunners are super speedy and can run up to 27 miles per hour.

SMALL BUT MIGHTY

These desert creepy-crawlies all have unique skills to help them survive in difficult conditions.

Big biters

Camel spiders use their scary jaws to attack bigger **PREY**, including lizards, snakes and birds!

Poo pushers

Dung beetles feed on the poo of other animals. Yuck! Some of them roll dung into balls, like this one.

Greedy guzzlers

Locusts can form enormous swarms and travel huge distances, eating every plant in their path.

A sting in the tail

Scorpions use the **VENOMOUS** sting at the end of their tails to hunt their prey.

Quick silver

These ants are covered in shiny hairs that reflect the sun, helping to keep them cool. They are also the fastest ants in the world!

BRILLIANT BURROWERS

It's cool to hang out underground! Many animals escape the heat of the desert by digging burrows to live in.

This meerkat is on guard duty, looking out for predators.

Pack members

Meerkats live together in groups called *packs*. They all share jobs between them.

Burrow for one

Bilbies like their space. They usually live alone and will have up to 12 burrows each!

Sand squatters

These owls like to take over burrows made by other animals.

The better to hear with

These big ears are great for listening out for prey.

Feisty felines

Sand cats may look like cute pets, but they are tough enough to handle extreme desert conditions.

GROWING GETS TOUGH

Most plants need lots of water to grow, but these plant don't mind dry weather.

Cacti

CLEVER CACTI

Cacti come in lots of different shapes and sizes. They store water in their stems and are covered in sharp spines.

PRETTY BUT PRICKLY

This funny looking cactus produces pretty flowers and edible fruit.

Prickly Pear Cactus

IT'S A DATE!

Date palms grow small fruits called dates that have been eaten by humans for many years.

PUTTING DOWN ROOTS

Joshua Trees have very deep roots to reach water hidden underground.

GETTING SAPPY

Agave have sweet sap inside their thick leaves.

PRECIOUS TREASURE

Not many types of flower grow in the desert.

MIGHTY MAMMALS

These MAMMALS are all tough enough to stand the heat of the desert.

LOOK BEHIND YOU!

Mountain lions like to sneak up on their prey, often jumping down on them from above.

BUTTING HEADS

Male bighorns will use their large, curly horns to fight each other, to prove who is strongest.

RARE RUNNERS

These rare gazelles are very good runners. They can reach speeds of 50 miles per hour.

SMELLS LIKE DINNER!

Coyotes have a great sense of smell to help them sniff out food from a long way away.

BIG BOUNCERS

Kangaroos don't walk, they jump! They have strong back legs to help them bounce over long distances.

WHERE IN THE WORLD?

KEY

= Desert Regions

This map shows all of the desert areas in the world. Not all deserts are the same. Different plants and animals are found in each one.

DID YOU KNOW?

Birds on the ground

Ostriches can't fly like other birds, but they can run really fast (up to 43 miles per hour)!

Mistaken identity

Camel Spiders are not actually spiders, although they are related to them.

Strength over size

If you compare size with strength, dung beetles are the world's strongest animal. They can pull up to 1,141 times their own bodyweight!

WHO WAS HIDING?

Did you spot the little egyptian tortoise playing hide-and-go-seek in each desert scene?

These tortoises live in desert areas in Egypt and Libya in North Africa.

They are very small and only grow to between 3 5 inches in length.

You would have a hard time finding these little creatures in real life. Although many are kept as pets, they are almost **EXTINCT** in the wild.

GLOSSARY

adapted (adaptation) - when a living thing has become able to survive in its surroundings by developing special features/skills over a long period of time.

burrow - a tunnel or hole in the ground made by an animal.

cold-blooded - animals with bodies that do not produce their own heat, and have to be heated or cooled by their surroundings.

endangered - if a type of animal or plant is in danger of dying out forever, then they are endangered.

extinct - when a type of plant or animal no longer exists anywhere in the world.

hibernate - Animals that hibernate spend all of their time sleeping during the winter and only wake up when it's warm again.

mammals - are animals with specific features. They all have hair or fur, drink milk from their mothers as babies, have a backbone and are warm-blooded.

nocturnal - Nocturnal animals sleep in the day and come out at night-time.

predator - an animal that hunts and kills other animals for food.

prey - an animal that is hunted by other animals for food.

reptiles - are animals with specific features. They have dry skin with scales, a backbone, breathe using lungs and they are cold-blooded (see above).

scavengers - don't hunt live animals. They eat animals that are already dead.

venomous - poisonous, or containing poison.

The Author

Annabel Griffin is a writer and artist based in the Southwest of England. She is passionate about nature and loves hiking and gardening. *What Can I See...?* is her first series of books for children.

The Illustrator

Rose Maclachlan is an illustrator based in Devon, who recently graduated from Falmouth University with a BA in Illustration. She likes to experiment with collage and texture to create her work and takes inspiration from her love of the outdoors and the beach.